10/05

Native American Life

The Southeast Indians

Daily Life in the 1500s

by Kathy Jo Slusher-Haas

Consultant:
Troy Rollen Johnson, PhD
American Indian Studies
California State University
Long Beach, California

Capstone *press*

Mankato, Minnesota

Bridgestone Books are published by Capstone Press,
151 Good Counsel Drive, P.O. Box 669, Mankato, Minnesota 56002.
www.capstonepress.com

Library of Congress Cataloging-in-Publication Data
Slusher-Haas, Kathy Jo.
    The Southeast Indians: daily life in the 1500s / by Kathy Jo Slusher-Haas.
    p. cm.—(Bridgestone books. Native American life)
    Summary: "A brief introduction to Native American tribes of the Southeast, including their social
structure, homes, clothing, food, and traditions"—Provided by publisher.
    Includes bibliographical references and index.
    ISBN 0-7368-4317-5 (hardcover)
    1. Indians of North America—Southern States—History—16th century—Juvenile literature.
2. Indians of North America—Southern States—Social life and customs—16th century—Juvenile
literature. 3. Southern States—Antiquities—Juvenile literature. I. Title. II. Series.
E78.S65S555 2006
975.004'97—dc22   2005001652

Editorial Credits
Christine Peterson, editor; Jennifer Bergstrom, set designer; Ted Williams, book designer;
    Jo Miller, photo researcher/photo editor; maps.com, map illustrator

Photo Credits
Art Resource, N.Y./Smithsonian American Art Museum, Washington, D.C., 12
Corbis/Bettmann, 16
Courtesy Frank H. McClung Museum. The University of Tennessee. Adapted with permission from
    paintings by Greg Harlin, cover, 6, 10
Creek Baskita Green Corn Ceremony, 1953/Fred Beaver, Creek-Seminole, 1911-1980/watercolor on
    paper/museum purchase/The Philbrook Museum of Art, Tulsa, Oklahoma. 1957.8, 18
Painting by Martin Pate, Newnan, Ga. Courtesy Southeast Archeological Center, National Park
    Service, 8, 14, 20

1 2 3 4 5 6 10 09 08 07 06 05

Table of Contents

Southeast
Tribal Areas in the 1500s

Legend

Mountain Range

River

Scale
Miles
0   50   100   150   200

0   100   200
Kilometers

Mississippi River

Appalachian Mountains

Cherokee

Cherokee   Catawba

Chickasaw

Creek   Yuchi
             Yamasee

Caddo

Choctaw

Natchez

Apalachee

Timucua

ATLANTIC OCEAN

GULF OF MEXICO

Seminole (1700s)

Calusa

4

The Southeast and Its People

When Spanish explorers arrived in the 1500s, Native Americans were **thriving** in the Southeast. The Southeast stretches from what is today the U.S. state of West Virginia, south to Florida, and west to eastern Texas. Mountains, valleys, and swamps cover the area.

Tribes had lived in this area for at least 5,000 years. They farmed, built homes, and hunted. Tribes often worked together to build homes and find food. Their daily life was shaped by the land around them.

◄ Traditional areas of Southeast tribes are shown over present-day borders.

Social Structure

In the Southeast, most people lived in family groups called **clans**. Clans lived together in villages. Villages were led by a chief and a group of elders.

Differences between clans often caused groups to form new tribes. In the 1700s, some Creek Indians formed a new tribe, called the Seminoles.

In clans, people worked together to get food. Men hunted. Women cooked meals. Everyone planted and harvested crops.

◀ In most Southeast tribes, chiefs and other leaders made decisions for the village.

Homes

Homes in the Southeast changed with the seasons. In summer, the Cherokee kept cool in homes made from clay. Layers of grass covered the roofs. In winter, they lived in round huts made of wood, mud, and grass.

Tribes built homes with materials they got from the land. The Creek lived in river valleys. They built huts with wood frames. Clay from rivers covered the walls. The Seminoles built homes, called chickees, on top of posts made from tree trunks. Chickees had grass roofs and wood frames, but no walls.

◄ Thick grass roofs covered most homes built by Southeast tribes.

Food

Land in the Southeast was good for farming. Tribes grew corn, beans, and squash. The Cherokee called these crops the "Three Sisters." Tribes ate these foods at most meals.

Tribes also hunted and gathered food in the woods. Men hunted deer, turkeys, and squirrels. Women cleaned the animals before cooking the meat. Women and children gathered honey, berries, sweet potatoes, and acorns.

◀ Women gathered and prepared nuts, berries, and other foods from Southeastern forests.

Clothing

Native Americans of the hot Southeast needed little clothing. Women wore skirts or dresses. Men wore **breechcloths** with a belt, leggings, and moccasins. Children often wore no clothes at all.

In the winter, the weather was cool. Most people wore warm robes made from buffalo, bear, or deer skins. Women sewed the skins together with bone needles and **sinew**.

◀ Boys in Southeast tribes sometimes wore breechcloths and moccasins made from animal skins.

Trading and Economy

Southeast Indians traded to get what they couldn't make or find in nature. They traded goods and shared ideas with other tribes.

Tribes living along the coast, like the Calusa, traded shells with inland tribes. Shells were used to make **wampum**. The Cherokee often used wampum belts to record laws and history.

Other tribes traded freshwater pearls, animal hides, maple syrup, and clay pipes. They traded these items for copper, iron, salt, and **flint**.

◄ The Calusa Indians collected shells from the ocean to make wampum for trade.

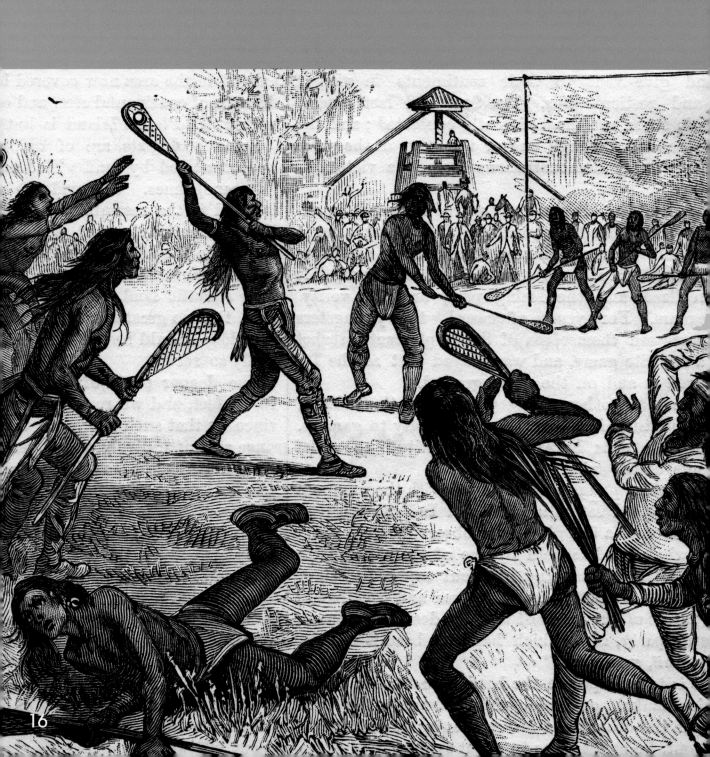

Leisure Time

Many Southeast tribes played outdoor games. Tribes often competed against each other. Stickball was a popular game. Tribes often played stickball to settle differences. Hundreds of players joined in a game. Players tossed a deerskin ball toward a goal using sticks with nets.

Chunkey was another popular game. The Choctaw played chunkey by rolling a stone down a field. Two players threw a pole where they thought the stone would stop. The pole closest to the stone won.

◄ Stickball is one of the earliest-known games played by Southeast tribes.

Traditions

Most tribes held **ceremonies** to honor nature. The Green Corn Ceremony celebrated the first corn harvest of the season. During this ceremony, people gave thanks for good crops and peace between tribes.

The ceremony also marked the start of a new year. During the celebration, tribes sang, danced, and held a feast. They also settled differences. Tribes lit a new fire as a sign that peace would continue.

◄ Southeast tribes celebrated a good corn harvest during the Green Corn Ceremony.

Passing On Traditions

In the 1500s, Southeast tribes did not have a written language. Tribes told stories to share their history. Elders used stories to explain how their tribes began. Other tales were about nature and the land.

Southeast Indians also used stories to teach others about their way of life. Through stories, people learned about the tribe's government and laws. They learned the importance of respect and bravery. In the Southeast, stories kept tribal history and traditions alive.

◄ Tribes often told stories to teach others about their past and traditions.

Glossary

breechcloth (BREECH-kloth)—a short, skirtlike garment that is tied around the waist and has open slits on the sides

ceremony (SER-uh-moh-nee)—formal actions, words, or music performed to mark an important occasion

clan (KLAN)—a large group of related families

flint (FLINT)—a very hard rock that produces sparks when struck with steel

sinew (SIN-yoo)—a strong piece of body tissue that connects muscle to bone

thrive (THRIVE)—to do well

tribe (TRIBE)—a group of people who share the same language and way of life

wampum (WAHM-puhm)—beads made from polished shells strung together or woven to make belts

Read More

Ansary, Mir Tamim. *Southeast Indians.* Native Americans. Des Plaines, Ill.: Heinemann, 2000.

Boraas, Tracey. *The Creek: Farmers of the Southeast.* American Indian Nations. Mankato, Minn.: Bridgestone Books, 2003.

Internet Sites

FactHound offers a safe, fun way to find Internet sites related to this book. All of the sites on FactHound have been researched by our staff.

Here's how:
1. Visit *www.facthound.com*
2. Type in this special code **0736843175** for age-appropriate sites. Or enter a search word related to this book for a more general search.
3. Click on the **Fetch It** button.

FactHound will fetch the best sites for you!

Index